DECORATING WITH

Funky Shui

DECORATING WITH Funky Shui

How to Lighten Up, Loosen Up, and Have Fun Decorating Your Home

Jennifer O'Neil and Kitty O'Neil

Andrews McMeel Publishing

Kansas City

Decorating with *Funky Shui*

04 05 06 07 08 KFO 10 9 8 7 6 5 4 3 2 1

Library of Congress Cataloging-in-Publication Data
O'Neil, Jennifer.
   Decorating with funky shui : how to lighten up, loosen up, and have fun decorating your home / Jennifer O'Neil and Kitty O'Neil.
      p. cm.
   ISBN: 0-7407-4199-3
     1. Feng shui. I. O'Neil, Kitty, 1965– II. Title.

BF1779.F4054 2004
133.3'337—dc22

2003064624

Photos by Kitty O'Neil, Jennifer O'Neil, and Margaret Dunne.

Some images copyright © 2003, 2004 by www.clipart.com.

Big Boy Bop on page 32 copyright © 1985 by John Baeder. Reprinted with permission.

Book design and composition by Holly Camerlinck.

We dedicate this book to our parents, **Jeanne and Larry O'Neil,** who raised us in a Funky Shui home before Funky Shui was cool.

Contents

Acknowledgments   ix

There's No Place Like Home   3

The **Living Room**: Live It Up   9

The **Kitchen**: Satisfy Your Hunger for Fun   25

The **Dining Room**:
Dine Without Reservations   43

The **Home Office**: All Work and No Play
Makes This a Dull Room   57

The **Bedroom**: An Altar to Love   73

The **Bathroom**:
Funky Shui = Funky + Water   89

The **Guest Room**: Wish You Were Here   103

The **Yard**: Don't Fence Me In   117

A Parting Gift   133

Acknowledgments

When we think about the friends and family members who have contributed to our expertise in Funky Shui and the making of this book, we get big cheesy grins and know we must give thanks.

For their contribution through material goods ranging from a life preserver to a six-foot Jack Skellington, we thank Ace Miles, Ashlyn Vincent, Bonnie and Don Miguel, Dan and Kate Marusich, Dimitri Proano, Don Takemura, Douglas and Kevina Vincent, Haven and Will Dubrul, Kathi Rose, Ken Brunt, Kristin Caudle, Luceti's Italian Restaurant, Jeannie Leahy, and Tom Anderson, aka Clutterboy.

For all the help we received in the production phase, we would like to recognize the fine attention to detail and quick turnaround of Bruce Turkel, Brant Smith, Connie Fox, Diane DiPrima, John P. Hunter, and Ron Sullivan. Thanks to Chris Hill, John Baeder, Anet James, and Ron Hemphill for allowing us to include their amazing art in our homes and our book. For welcoming us into the world of publishing and making this book a reality, we acknowledge our agent, Sheree Bykofsky; Megan Buckley; Janet Rosen; our editor, Jennifer Fox; designer Holly Camerlinck; and the whole Andrews McMeel clan.

We'd like to especially thank Margaret Dunne, who took many of the photographs in the book.

For their inspiration and support, we thank Ed Hoffman, Pam Harmell, Rose Barry, John Hill, Lauri Berkenkamp, Clark O'Neil, Kevin O'Neil, Renée O'Neil, Larry O'Neil, and Jeanne O'Neil. For letting us decorate our homes with tcha tcha tchotchkes, we thank Joseph Knight and Rand Hill.

DECORATING WITH Funky Shui

MYSTERY SPOT
SANTA CRUZ CA

There's No Place Like Home

If *Feng Shui* is the art of arranging objects to promote harmony, then *Funky Shui* is the art of arranging objects to make your home and your life fun. With a carefree attitude and an eye toward your playful good taste, Funky Shui shows you how to lighten up, loosen up, and have fun decorating your home. By combining color, lighting, and an abundance of favorite things into off-the-wall themed rooms, you can bring the magic of Funky Shui into your home.

In Feng Shui, furniture arrangement and object placement can cause positive energy to flow throughout a home. If, for example, your house is poorly sited on "the back of the Dragon," only some serious Feng Shui can rescue your Chi from his scaly crabbiness.

Funky Shui also utilizes furniture and object placement, but tames the Dragon by amusing him in a playful vortex of fun. Funky Shui shows you how to bring fun and imagination back into your home. If you begin losing fun energy through the back door, Funky Shui might advise you to block its escape with a trio of alert lawn penguins.

For many people, decorating is a chore with rigid rules and little imagination. Why strive to follow the trends when "simple living" is simply boring? To the Funky Shui master, simple living boils down to simple fun. More fun in the house promotes more fun in your life. If you boxed up travel souvenirs and photos from your honeymoon in the Big Apple, you're stifling your *Honeymoon Mojo*. And that generic art from Pottery Barn is squeezing out space for your own precious memories. With Funky Shui, your mementos aren't packed away on the top shelf of the guest room closet; they live on your mantelpiece—fun and center! Be reminded of your trip to the Bahamas, not the last time you shopped at Bed Bath & Beyond.

Previous left: Invite your toys out of the closet. You don't have to be a kid to have a playroom!

Previous right: There's no place like the Funky Shui home!

Left: Funky Shui is as easy as 1-2-3 — lawn penguins, that is.

Below left: Don't stifle your *Honeymoon Mojo!* Display your souvenirs on your mantel, fun and center.

Below: Hula Nodders are a Tahitian Treat.

How does one practice the art of Funky Shui?

Start with the *fun*-damentals, some clever tools, and a fresh attitude. Using the Four Fundamental Directions of Funky Shui, you can steer your home decorating toward the light. When you're surrounded by lighthearted fun and whimsy, you can't help but take it in. We call this "enlightenment." Each chapter takes you through the Fun-damentals, the Four Directions of Funky Shui.

1. **Find the Playful Center:** Create a conversation piece.
2. **Color Me Funky:** Brighten up with color.
3. **Enlighten-up:** Light up your life with delightful lighting.
4. **Abundance Through Abundance:** Celebrate your favorite things.

Time to bring it all together. Take a look around the house. Is your kitchen suffering from *Simple Living*? Time to dig the snow globe collection out of the attic. Forty-seven snow globes are like travel trophies that represent joy and adventure (and no two are alike). Don't have a snow globe collection? With Funky Shui, where there's a will there's eBay! Even the amateur practitioner of Funky Shui can cause mysterious heavenly forces to align and bring fun home. Now break out your metal lunchbox collection, twinkle lights, and those collector spoons from forty-three states, and let's have some fun.

Far left: Stable labels and Astroturf make this an OK corral. Giddyap!

Left: Get out those snow globes and the forecast is fun.

the LiVING ROOM

Live It Up

What's the most public space in the house, the one room every visitor except the meter reader will see? The living room, your shrine to entertainment. This room is all about leisure and amusement and, as such, is the life force of fun for the whole house.

As both a public and private space, the living room is the external incarnation of your inner spirit, reflecting your most playful self. Your living room doesn't have to be a stilted furniture showroom with store-bought taste. Instead, make it a *living* room full of fresh fun with a big dash of you. To bring your room to life, apply the Four Fun-damental Directions of Funky Shui.

Find the Playful Center

Start a Conversation

The conversation piece is an ancient tool of Funky Shui used to focus attention on fun. Have you ever been to a garage sale or a junk shop and seen a mannequin or a traffic light for sale? "What a cool object," you might have thought, "but where would I put it?" In the Funky Shui living room, of course. Every room could use a large unusual item to put an exclamation point on it. (If you find a neon exclamation point, all the better!) When everything in a room is the same scale, it can become repetitive and boring. A focal point anchors a room in oceans of fun.

Previous: Come on, take a chance! A Funky Shui living room can be *slots of fun!*

Above left: This focal point gives your living room a little oompah-pah.

Above right: Birds of Paradise sing in a gilded birdcage. Talk about a conversation piece!

Right: A movie star cutout can be the star of your living room. (And *this* cardboard canine is housebroken.)

Did you inherit Granddad's tuba? What luck! Place it on a stand with big wire musical notes shooting straight up from the middle of the horn; stick in a few ostrich plumes and wood scrolls to create an amazing *objet d'art* that is a Saul Steinberg cartoon come to life. A tuba that looks like it's always playing creates a symphony of happiness! Or gild a fancy birdcage and give it a place of prominence. Not sure what to put in it? How about some flowers? Birds-of-paradise, of course. Paint a cow skull with vibrant colors. Didn't find a cow skull on your hike? Then make one out of papier-mâché. If Martha were funky, that's what she would do.

Conversation pieces come in all shapes and sizes: a wall of old license plates, a framed theater poster from your favorite movie, your name spelled out in mismatched store sign letters, a shadow-box coffee table displaying the first issue of *Wonder Woman* (plus a pair of her gold cuffs). The sky's the limit, which means the focal point doesn't have to sit on the floor, table, or shelf. Hang a dragon kite across the ceiling. Now that's taming the Dragon!

The Funky Shui practitioner selects a conversation piece using the trinity of *Big, Funky,* and *Different:*

Think Big: A great flea market find could be a large focal point. An oversized wire mesh shoe says, "I like shoes and the bigger the better!" Imagine a totem pole from floor to ceiling.

Think Funky: An ordinary grandfather clock can become a stunning conversation piece with the addition of rhinestones. Put the "ut" in "utterly ut." You can buy a cardboard cutout of your favorite movie star. Nothing like a life-size Steve Martin to center your fun around.

Think Different: Hound Dog Andirons are great for a dog lover. A crystal ball in the center of your living room infuses your life with mystery. A fortune-telling machine brings fun and fortune and more than a little conversation. An old store mannequin can be dressed up for any occasion. Even chess sets come in Funky Shui varieties, from *Alice in Wonderland* to *Star Wars*.

When you think conversation piece, think of something people would *talk* about. One postcard of Pasadena on the wall may drum up a single comment, but one hundred framed postcards of Prague on the wall and you've started a conversation. Come out of your cocoon by dangling large paper butterflies from the ceiling in even-numbered rows. If butterflies in your tummy are a sign of impending thrills, imagine what a room full of paper monarchs can do for your life!

Color Me Funky

It Doesn't Have to Match Your Sofa

"Live in a beige house, live a beige life." Or so the saying goes. Okay, we made that up, but it should be a saying, along with "Add color to your living room, add color to your life."

Perhaps you're feeling ready to break the "white walls barrier," but you're not sure where to start. Find a swatch of fabric you like and challenge yourself to use all the colors in it. Even if you only use the cloth on a throw pillow in your living room, all the colors already go together. A ready-made palette. What freedom!

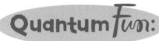

Quantum *Fun*:

Kid's Art + Frame + Easel
= Museum of
Really Modern Art

Above: Framing your child's painting makes your home the Museum of *Really* Modern Art.

Mix It Up with Intoxicating Colors for Your Living Room

Mint Julep: Makes happy hour last all night, just add an umbrella.

Black and Tan: Hops up your living room.

Lemon and Lime: Adds a little sprite to your life.

Tangerine Scream: Tells people, "I'm not afraid to paint my living room orange."

Avoid a Hangover from These Regrettable Color Schemes

Scotch and Milk: This beige will leave a bad taste in your mouth.

Avocado Colada: A color scheme that doesn't go down easy.

Quantum *Fun*:

For proof that the *fun* is greater than the sum of its parts, display objects of the same color together. How about a photograph of a fire hydrant, red candles, and a Matchbox fire truck to spark up an inferno of fun?

Above left: Break the "white walls barrier" and color me fun!

Above right: Somebody call 9-1-1, 'cause this all-red grouping is H-O-T!

Shirley Temple Black: A cloying cocktail gone to the dark side.

Clamato Cocktail: Quarantine this color scheme!

Once you have your paint chips, don't be afraid to paint the walls. All of them. Seriously. In Funky Shui, a room of all white absorbs joy. A cream pillow on a white sofa in an eggshell room may look modern and dramatic but it lacks flavor. According to Funky Shui Color Theory, walls painted vivid colors intensify the joy. Paint one wall lime, three walls blue, and be amazed at the energy you can create for $50 worth of latex enamel. Once

Above left: Let your skeletons out of the closet. A "Day of the Dead" collection gives this room new life.

Above right: The devil's in the details.

Far right: One candle may light the way, but a dozen candles leads to *funlightenment.*

you've taken the plunge, picking out throw pillows will be a snap. And speaking of throw pillows, ever see fantastic buttons you couldn't possibly wear? Put 'em on your cushions to button-up good taste. Trim those plain pillows with beads and fringe and tassels. A letter per pillow could spell out your favorite word or saying. How about "R-E-L-A-X" or "S-I-T"?

Enlighten-up
Trip the Light Fantastic

Now it's time to add light and life to your living room. Candles can be a funky way to add coziness, and don't forget the warm glow of a fireplace around the winter holidays. But how can you increase the glow and let the fun flow winter, spring, summer, and fall? Vintage flickering logs plugged into

LOUNGE

Above: This lamp will lighten up any room.

Right: Add roses to dress up your run-of-the-mill wood mirror.

your fireplace will light up your smile 365 days a year. And why save Christmas lights for the tree? Call them "twinkle lights" and you can use them year-round. Scatter yellow twinkle lights along the top of your mantel to add a little magic to your hearth. A string of fruit lights can add a little Carmen Miranda to your Juicy Fruit Living Room. Or try a giant letter "K" that stands for "kooky." If you really want to revitalize your living room, go back to where all the fun began, with antique illuminated store signs. Nothing says funky like the letters "F-U-N-K-Y" in glowing red neon!

Task lighting in the form of lamps on your end tables is functional, but it can also be funky. A retro rocket ship lamp is out of this world, while a hula girl motion lamp says *mahalo* when you turn it on. Why not monkey around with palm tree monkey lamps? The old adage is true: You can't have too many monkey lamps.

A framed mirror over the mantel reflects fun into your room and into your life, especially if the frame is more than a run-of-the-mill wood number. A dozen faux roses around that mirror will make your room blossom. Oversized gilding can make a mirror (or any framed piece) fit for the National Gallery. Don't have a gilded frame? Add huge crown molding and spray paint it gold. And just for good measure, frost a few words across the looking glass, like "Objects in mirror may be closer than they appear."

Finally, a word about spotlights: "Yes!" Funky is a feature when shown in the right light. A spot can hang on a wall and light up your

Parlor Trick:

A disco ball in your living room is a party that's always happening.

Mona Lisa. A spot can hang from the ceiling and illuminate your life-size carousel horse. A spot can even sit on the floor and light up your six-foot boot from Ye Olde Boot Shop. Go, Spot, go!

Abundance Through Abundance
Tcha Tcha Tchotchkes

Perhaps the most important element of the Art of Funky Shui is known as "stuff." Tchotchkes, bric-a-brac, keepsakes, collectibles (disparagingly referred to by the Dragon as *dust collectors* or *clutter*), whatever you call them, they symbolize abundance. While *Architectural Digest* would have you hide

your collections and donate your souvenirs to Goodwill, Funky Shui celebrates your stuff. The mementos you pick up during your travels remind you of your fun vacation. *Souvenir* means *remember,* after all. And the special items you search for at eBay and the Antique Faire not only provide insight into who you are, but they also remind

Left: Life is a merry-go-round. (But in a good way.)

Above: Shake it up!

you of your passions. Make a beloved collection part of your decor, and your home will reflect your inner fun.

Got three of something? Then you've got a collection! Your weakness for LEGOs, whether you are eight or eighty-eight, brings your inner child out to play. Show off your penchant for gumball machines, your fanaticism for trading cards, or your passion for piggy banks. Put the pedal to the metal and let your Matchbox cars race on a track through your living room.

An amazing collection can be a conversation piece because nothing creates a buzz like one hundred Pez dispensers. Collecting toys isn't just for kids, and what better way to nurture your inner child. (Plus grown-ups get a bigger allowance!)

Funky Shui Toy Collections

> ***Happy Meal Toys:*** Anything with *happy* in the title brings luck and joy.
>
> ***Cartoon Collectibles:*** Frequent exposure to humor is good for your Chi.
>
> ***Vintage Cracker Jack Prizes:*** Like the pearl inside an oyster they bring happiness (and temporary tattoos!).
>
> ***Classic Wind-up Toys:*** Wind them all up at once to help you unwind.

Left: Build a conversation piece out of your love of LEGO.

Above: Your parlor is a perfect place for a parade of Pez!

Quantum *Fun*:

Ungrouped items = clutter,
Grouped items =
conversation piece

Top: Fill a giant shoe with Happy Meal Toys for a big case of Happy Feet.

Bottom: Comic strip collectibles create smiles for miles. The funnies aren't called that for nothin'.

Inset: Collectibles are like cows. They naturally herd.

Far right: Got three? It's a collection. Got a hundred? You've got Funky Shui!

The way you display your collection can raise it to the level of art or lower it to the level of junk. A proper display gives your collectibles importance and stature. Try facing your items the same way to organize them; for example, a herd of mini-cows looking in the same direction looks tidy, and makes guests wonder what they're all lookin' at.

If your collection takes over the room, go with the Funky Shui flow and transform that room with the thematic power of your collection. Love the movies? Center your room around your favorite film. Start with the movie poster and ticket stubs, then head to eBay for the lobby card, press kit, and other movie memorabilia. If luck is truly on your side and the Dragon gives your movie pick two thumbs

up, you may even find a mint condition premiere ticket.

Hollywood not your cup of grande half-caf mocha latte? Any collection can make a great theme. Love baseball collectibles? Create your own dugout and take yourself out to the ball game every day. Is your last name Knight? Then hold court in your own Camelot with a collection of knights, including a life-size knight in shining armor. Are you a cat lady? Go into a feline frenzy and create the *purrfect* room full of your kitty-cat collectibles. There's never a lull in the conversation in a Funky Shui living room.

Right: Make your favorite collection a focal point and gain abundance through abundance.

theKiTChEN

Satisfy Your Hunger for Fun

The kitchen is the center of the home. It's the heart of the party even when the chips and salsa are in the living room. An appetizing kitchen is rich, fresh, and flavorful, and that doesn't just apply to the food. A kitchen decorated with your favorite things brings more fun into the heart of the house and radiates joy to the corners of your home. To meet the RDAF (Recommended Daily Allowance of Funky), apply the Four Fun-damental Directions of Funky Shui.

Find the Playful Center
Open Twenty-four Hours

Late-night snackers know where to find the playful center of the kitchen, even in the dark. It's the refrigerator, known in some schools of Funky Shui as "The Fridge." Whether yours is trendy steel, clean white, or '60s avocado, The Fridge is the protector of your family's *Food Shui*, so its placement is key. However, in-depth international studies have determined that hauling your 200-pound refrigerator all over the kitchen, scraping your checkerboard linoleum and giving you a hernia, is

TODAY'S SPECIALS

Rainbow Ham
Slug Casserole
Hot Mayonnaise Pie
Snail Shakes

bad Funky Shui. Therefore, it is declared that the current placement of your refrigerator is ideal, because moving it could displace your kitchen's good *foodju*.

In this case, the placement of your playful center is not as important as its adornment. Consider your fridge a giant magnetic easel just waiting to become an artful shrine to happiness and healthy appetites. Hanging snapshots of family, friends, and pets on the refrigerator is encouraged. Like leaving guitar picks on Buddy Holly's grave, covering your fridge with family mementos is a way to honor and remember them, even if they live just next door. Use your fridge to display your daughter's A+ essay on her goldfish, your Aunt Dottie's recipe for snicker-doodles, and your collection of state map postcards. Care should be taken to cover every exposed surface of your fridge, as each item placed

Rule of *Fun*:

Post no bills.
And by bills we mean what you owe American Express.

Far Left: Hey, Mom! What's for supper?

Left: Alphabet magnets are good for a spell of fun.

Above: This is a fine example of animal magnetism.

Above: Send the most important appliance in the house a postcard. "Wish you were here!"

Right: A collection of state magnets tells the universe you haven't yet been to Hawaii yet. A good message to send.

on its shell is an offering to the Gods of Good Taste (or at least what tastes good). Display report cards (if they're good), photos of your trip to the Alamo (Remember? The Alamo?), and your family's activity calendar (only for the fun stuff—no chores!).

Certain items are more appropriate than others for your fridge adornment. *Do* post your son Bill's red-and-yellow crayon drawing of your dog Sparkplug. (Pets are the official mascots of

Funky Shui.) *Don't* post photos of supermodels from *Cosmo* unless you are male, single, and in your twenties. For people on diets, these photos anger the Food Gods, forcing them to send bad *foodju* your way in the form of Rice Krispy Treats free for the taking at the office.

Enhance *funlightenment* by adhering offerings to the refrigerator with entertaining magnets. Try state magnets to invoke travel, veggie magnets because vegetables are good for you, plastic conversation hearts to keep communication flowing, or doggie-dress-up magnetic paper dolls because it's darn funny to dress up a rottweiler in an off-the-shoulder pink chiffon evening gown. Make ordinary magnetic poetry more Funky Shui by using Yiddish words ('cause in

Funky Shui everything rhymes with tchotchke), or by creating your own words with magnetic strips and a Sharpie (perfect for adding your favorite made-up words, like *beautimus, fabtastic,* and *bazillion* to your poetic palette).

Funambulism:

There's a fine line to walk when choosing funky magnetic words for your fridge. Eliminate words like *somber, pallid,* or *weep*. Replace them with fabulous Funky Shui words like *shiny, swirling,* and *candy*.

The top of The Fridge is the crown of the kitchen's playful center and is, therefore, a perfect location for shrines to epicureans like Julia Child, Emeril Lagasse, or Betty Crocker. To create an effective tribute to Betty Crocker, display a color page from one of her "Fabulous Fifties" cookbooks (choosing a recipe that lists lard as the first ingredient will make all of your recipes seem low-fat). Place the framed recipe page on a plate stand on the top of your fridge next to your old Easy Bake Oven to bring the good *foodju* into your saucepan and encourage kitchen experimentation. Making up recipes that pose as real recipes is the pinnacle of Funky Shui. Create recipe cards with directions for Lemon-Lime Lamb or Crown Roast of Hot Dogs (rumor has it this one's real). That's a recipe for fun.

food Shui:

A plant placed on the top of a fridge feeds the air, but take care not to use an edible plant as its placement in the kitchen could put it on the defensive, thus upsetting nutritional balance.

Be careful to store only foods you like in your fridge, for bad foods cause bad moods—and that's not Funky Shui. Leftovers should be stored in the refrigerator only if they are going to be eaten. Remember: Leftovers are welcome in a Funky Shui home. *Guilt*overs are not. All foods should remain tightly covered, for naked food leaves you exposed to fungus, which may

Left: A fridge-top shrine to Betty Crocker guarantees good cookin'.

Above: Light a candle to protect your soufflé from the Failed Recipe Gnomes.

contain the word *fun,* but it's not. Take care to remove foods before they turn because stinky foods are *Funk* Shui and, well, that's a whole other book.

Foods for the Funky Shui Fridge

- Cookie Dough
- Reddi wip
- Maraschino Cherries
- Chocolate Sauce

Forbidden Foods for the Funky Shui Fridge

- Tupperware Science Project
- Liquid Lettuce
- Desiccated Carrot
- Cough Syrup

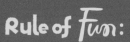

Rule of *Fun*:

Throw away millennium fruitcake, as ancient food buildup clogs your freezer's good energy.

Color Me Funky

Thirty Wonderful Flavors

Painting your kitchen an appealing color is a recipe for appetizing meals through the Palette/Palate Connection. The key to finding the right color for your kitchen walls is to think *yummy*.

Tasty Colors for Your Kitchen

Apricot Nectar: Creates an ambrosia of joy in your kitchen.

Candy Apple: A candy apple a day keeps the Dragon away.

Buttercream Icing: Spreads creamy sweetness throughout your kitchen.

Banana Cream Pie: In your face fun!

Unappetizing Colors for Your Kitchen

Wheat Grass: Looks as bad as it tastes.

Melba Toast: This crumby color is tasteless.

Brussels Sprout: Even the dog won't like it.

Gasping Grouper: This color stinks!

Left: Big Boys guard your kitchen from the food snobs.

Colors That Sound Yummy, but Look Yucky

Pâté de Foie Gras: Sounds good, but do you know what this is?!

Pumpkin Pie: If you've had a baby, you'll know why.

Mustard: Unless your decor is "Late '60s Revival."

Nougat: A sweet name for *Taupe*.

Once you've selected the food color that whets your appetite, choose dishtowels, trivets, and oven mitts that will carry out your tasty color scheme. Decorative curtains guard your family's food from theft (think of all the pies that have been stolen from windowsills!). Coordinating oven mitts provide aesthetic harmony and protection against harmful forces that can burn fingers. Matching trivets safeguard your counters and may even ward off the Failed Recipe Gnomes. If you are lucky enough to have inherited putty, avocado, or harvest gold appliances, use the dominant color as your starting point and create a theme. Why fight fate when new appliances are so expensive?

Use art to add even more color to your kitchen. Fruit crate labels are inexpensive, food related, and funky. Go for hilarious brands like *Up and Atom Carrots, Yum Yum Apples,* and *Buxom Melons*. Or make your own labels, like *Insipid Brand Carrots* featuring cute little bunnies or *Meadowlark Lemons* featuring a singing bird (or a Globetrotter). It is so inspiring to think of *World Peas*.

Top: Crate labels are fun. Made-up crate labels are funny.

Right: Don't leave these collectibles cooped up! Let these roosters strut their stuff in your Kitchen-Doodle-Doo.

Spotlight on the Kitchen

Bright lighting is essential to cooking in the Funky Shui home because ample light ensures minimal mix-ups. No one wants catnip in the spaghetti sauce (except, of course, the cat). Funky Shui texts advise that sharp objects be wielded only in the brightest of light. Mood lighting in the kitchen is appropriate only when the cooking is complete, for soft lighting can hide even the biggest kitchen mess from your dining room guests.

Hang a row of sunshine string-lights under your stove's hood to make every day sunny. Couple them with

Rule of *Fun* :

Number birthday candles are *not* Funky Shui.

· ·

Above: Sunny twinkle lights let the sunshine in.

Right: Birthday candles aren't just for birthdays anymore.

your collection of rooster trivets, water jugs, and knickknacks, and you'll awaken each day to a hearty "Cock-a-doodle-doo." In the kitchen, roosters serve and protect your roost from the scorches of life experience and the flames of the Dragon.

Candles are more than mood-makers. When placed in the kitchen, a candle becomes a powerful talisman against bad *foodju,* best demonstrated by burning a candle to the right of the cutting board while chopping an onion. Anything from a simple white votive to an elaborate candelabra will do. The flame extinguishes the toxic fumes from the injured onion, thus scaring off bad *foodju* (and sparing your mascara).

Birthday candles are not just for birthday cakes anymore. Why save those delightful mini-tapers for special annual occasions? Feel special every day by placing one birthday candle in the center of your Twinkie. A birthday candle transforms a muffin into a healthy cupcake. Your birth was a special event to be celebrated throughout the year. Use ballerina candleholders with multi-colored spiral candles to create your own private performance of *The Nutcracker*.

A functioning light in your refrigerator is key to ensuring the balance of Funky Shui in the kitchen and the home. This light represents the soul of your playful center and serves as feedback to your food needs. But remember, opening the refrigerator door more than twenty-four times in a twenty-four hour period could awaken the Dragon and force him to eat your leftover filet mignon from your favorite Japanese steakhouse. Bad *foodju*.

Abundance Through Abundance
Kitchen Kitsch

To encourage abundance in your kitchen, consider it your own personal horn-o-plenty. Not only is your kitchen overflowing with fruits and vegetables, it's filled with your favorite kitchen kitsch.

SPICE OF LIFE · HAND PICKED · LAUGHTER OF MAIDENS · WT. 1.8 OZ. (51 GRAM

SPICE OF LIFE · HAND PICKED · SEEDS-O-CHANGE · WT. 1.8 OZ. (51 GRAM

SPICE OF LIFE · HAND PICKED · NEW LEAVES · WT. 1.8 OZ. (51 GRAM

SPICE OF LIFE · HAND PICKED · CARE-AWAY SEEDS · WT. 1.8 OZ. (51 GRAM

SPICE OF LIFE · HAND PICKED · SMILE SPRINKLES · WT. 1.8 OZ. (51 GRAM

SPICE OF LIFE · HAND PICKED · EXTRA TIME · WT. 1.8 OZ. (51 GRAM

Clearly labeled spice jars are important for clarity while cooking. Spice jars with made-up labels like "Essence of Butterflies," "Care-Away Seeds," and "Some Like It Hot" season your kitchen with laughter. How about gathering together your salt and pepper shakers? Nothing says spicy living like twenty pairs of ceramic souvenirs serving up a dash of flavor. A collection of tiny teapots staves off the tempest. Beer steins from around the globe represent world harmony and encourage harmony within your world.

Hang exactly five copper pots, bottoms facing east, to produce a perpetual patina of positive energy throughout the kitchen. To

Left: Nothing says spicy living like a seasoned salt and pepper collection.

Above: These original varieties are the spice of life.

establish a "clarity corner," create a vivid vignette in your kitchen by gathering seven items of the same color. For example, place seven cobalt blue glass bottles in a row on your kitchen windowsill. They look so cute, why not put a single daisy in each one?

Matching coffee, flour, and sugar canisters ensure your baking balance while guarding your powdered goods from critter-invasion. Every Funky Shui home requires at least one cookie jar, preferably in the shape of Cookie Monster, the Pillsbury Dough-boy, or a giant Oreo. Release the fear of getting caught with your

hand in the cookie jar by placing it out in the open and encouraging your family to snack whenever they'd like. This is about
fun (and cookies), after all.

Many Funky Shui novices ask, "What makes a good fruit
bowl?" A Funky Shui question for the ages. The answer? Almost
anything. A vintage aluminum colander with three tiny legs makes
a great fruit bowl for your Old-Fashioned Farmhouse Kitchen. Has

Hang autographed black-and-
white 8 x 10s of celebrities in
silver frames around the top of
your kitchen to capture the
mood of a good diner and
ensure good dining. If you do
not have 8 x 10s of celebrities,
take headshots of your friends
and have them autograph each
photo to you ("All my best,
Bobby Schwartzberg"). If you
have more than a few carnival
caricatures, frame them and
put them up. Instant Sardi's!

Left: If it's concave, it's a fruit bowl!

The Dragon and the Kitchen:

The Dragon can easily be sated in the kitchen with a party tray of finger foods and petits fours. Small foods are Funky Shui. Add a frilly toothpick and . . . well, need we say more?

your punch bowl been to any parties lately? How about putting it to work as a glamorous fruit bowl? Want something more fun and funky? A footed chalice, a small birdbath, half a globe (the bottom half with the stand, preferably—no need to turn the world upside down for a bunch of bananas). How about a small galvanized steel washtub? If it's concave, consider it a fruit bowl.

Everyone knows that a good cup of coffee serves up good *Jojo Mojo*. Like the rising sun, it brings warmth, clarity, and energy to the home. Decorative coffee cups find the perfect home in the Funky Shui kitchen on a shelf over the sink. And there's nothing like starting your Funky Shui day with a cup of good mojo in your Funky Shui kitchen.

Above: You don't have to turn the world upside-down for a banana.

the DiNING ROOM

Dine Without Reservations

Wine and dine! Every room in the Funky Shui home deserves to fulfill its purpose, so don't just save this room for Turkey Day. The dining room is for dining. Get the best table in the house by following the Four Fun-damental Directions of Funky Shui.

Find the Playful Center
A Table Set for Fun

Think a dining room set has to look like something you won on *Let's Make a Deal*? Think outside the box. Your dining table can be made of just about anything as long as it's flat on one side and bigger than a plate or two. A frosted glass top on a column is clearly funky. A big barn door just needs four legs to become a rustic table for hearty home-cookin'. Come and get it! For a sacred supper, try a stained-glass church door resting on some saintly statuary. Or paint your old wood table with permanent faux placemats and antique lace.

Some dining tables just need a makeover to revive their faded glory. Instead of trashing the ugly old thing, dress it up in a red-and-white tablecloth. Add a Chianti candle and your family will say,

"Mama Mia, thatsa bella dining room!" Don't disappoint your dining table by thinking only decorator stripes and florals. Your table wants a new set of clothes. Denying her could set the Dragon on a shopping spree, and that's not good for your profit zone.

Think zebra stripes have no place in the dining room? They set the stage for bamboo-handled flatware, woven placemats, and a chandelier festooned with monkeys (okay, maybe not real monkeys). A bold '60s op-art pattern of magenta and orange with red dots makes all the other decorating decisions for you. Your table is feeling very fashionable. (She thanks you.)

Sometimes the table stifles entertainment energies. So don't be afraid to take the table out and make room for a rainy-day picnic *without* the ants. Scatter pillows on the floor for sushi night (be sure to leave your shoes outside). Or have popcorn and pizza on a floor covered in sleeping bags for girls'-night fun. Attire? Footie pajamas, please.

In the Funky Shui home, all table shapes are welcome and celebrated as each unique shape brings an important element into the dining room:

Round: Reflects the never-ending circle of love that you share in your home. Plus no one has to sit at the head of the table.

Square: Brings an even amount of the four directions to the table, encouraging symmetry and board games. (And by placing a square in your home, you guarantee you're not a square.)

Oval: Allows for even circulation of Chi and easy passing of Cheesy Potatoes.

Rectangular: Shaped like a brick, representing the brick and mortar connectedness of your home. Plus this shape is easy to find, which saves time for fun.

Chairs are the often-overlooked cohabitants of the dining room. But chairs make the dining experience complete. (This isn't a Stand-N-Snack, unless, of course, you choose that as your dining room theme.) Your dining room chairs don't have to match. You can pick up funky, one-of-a-kind chairs at thrift shops, antique stores, and garage sales till you have all the chairs you need. Combine them with an amazing collection of unique plates, stemware, and flatware and you've created a kooky-chic dining

After-Dinner Hint:

A Funky Shui dining room attracts off-hours visitors and between-meal snackers, making your dining room fun 24/7.

Left: Dine without reservations. ("Mama Mia, thatsa fun dining room!")

Above: It's the Leaning Tower of Cheesa!

room. You'll feel like royalty with a throne at the head of the table. ("Please pass the macaroni and cheese, Your Majesty.")

Color Me Funky
Off with White

Gild that lily! The dining room can have the greatest flexibility of any room in the home if you embrace playfulness through color. Tablecloths, placemats, napkins, plates, glasses, and table runners are all color-fun tools for changing your dining room from the *Last Supper* to *Breakfast at Tiffany's*. And you can change your dining room color schemes as often as Barbie changes her clothes. Be daring and mix a red tablecloth with marigold plates and nap-

kins. Or go ultramodern with matte black square plates on a glass table. A table runner in Chinese red satin invites the Dragon to dinner. Fortune: Your future is looking funky!

Delicious Colors for Your Dining Room

Cherries Jubilee: Stay home and paint the town red.

Salmon: Have salmon-chanted evening every night.

Chardonnay: Cheers to fabulous dining.

Cordon Bleu: Bon appétit!

Icky Colors for Your Dining Room

Cottage Cheese: Like being on a low-color diet.

Grease: A good musical, a bad color scheme.

Fish Bone: Don't get caught with this boring beige.

Liver and Onions: Yuck!

After-Dinner Hint:

Occasional chairs can be used occasionally.

● ● ● ● ● ● ● ● ● ● ● ● ● ● ● ● ●

Left: Bring the picnic inside and you can have fun rain or shine.

Above: Indoor Picnic, BYOA: Bring Your Own Ants.

Top: You can play with your food when you have mah-jongg chopstick rests.

Above: You say "tomato," we say "centerpiece."

Above right: Sprinkle your dining room with color.

For an infusion of color in the center of your table, choose a centerpiece that matches the flavor of your dining room theme. A two-foot-tall glass vase with three dozen long-stemmed red roses is Opening Night Chic. *Bravo!* For extra romance, sprinkle red and pink rose petals around your place settings. Rose petals

are nature's colorful confetti. Never got around to taking that floral arranging class? You can create something spectacular without a degree—just add imagination. An aluminum watering can loaded with Gerbera daisies completes your Garden Party. Or try a collection of mason jars featuring one giant mum each. A centerpiece doesn't have to be floral. A cactus garden sets the table for your Southwestern Soiree *sans* tumbleweeds. Create a rock garden to complement the Japanese takeout. Place a glass bowl of ripe red cherries in the center of your table (because that old saying is true).

Above: Mums in mason jars make every meal marvelous.

Enlighten-up
Chandeliers of Merriment

Chandeliers formalize funky fun, especially when decorated with Funky Shui. Start with any hanging lighting fixture, then turn on the fun. You don't have to go broke to make it baroque. A tulip tole pendant is not just your garden-variety chandelier. Add extra crystals to maximize magic. Hang heart-shaped ornaments for a year-round look of love. And remember those fake fruits in the fruit bowl? Wouldn't they look sweet up there with the electric candles?

Adjust the ambiance in your dining room every night to go with your menu. Just thread a white feather boa through your chandelier for a black-tie dinner. A strand of pearls is perfect on Oyster Night. Having Tex-Mex? String red-hot chili pepper lights through the swags of the chandelier for a Fiesta del Funky. Colorful skeleton maracas shake up the mood, while you sip margaritas and dip nachos. All you need now is a mariachi band to get the party started. *Olé!*

Funambulism:

A dimmer on your chandelier walks a fine line between enhancing romance and obscuring fish bones. Use with caution.

Left: Let a chandelier shine the light of fun on your Funky Shui dinner party.

Top: Make your chandelier say *Olé!* for a Fiesta del Funky.

Above: Your chandelier will light up the room when you dress it for dinner.

Don't yet have a ceiling fixture you like? Then you're in luck. Here's permission to get a new one. A massive medieval chandelier keeps you illuminated in the Dark Ages. How about some matching wall sconces? Want to go even more rustic? Heavy old crossbeams with thick flame-shaped bulbs will make you want to eat with your hands.

Abundance Through Abundance
The Best Table in the House

A rich theme nourishes your *foodju*. So try a diner theme, like Blue Plate Special. Placemats made from Boomerang Formica can

Top left: Have a swinging good time with multicolor drink monkeys.

Top center: Pearls are perfect for oysters on the half shell.

Top right: Deck the halls with boughs of jolly.

Above: Looks like we've got visitors.

showcase cafeteria plates. Season your meatloaf with stainless-steel-and-glass salt and pepper shakers. (For real authenticity, add a few grains of uncooked rice in the salt shaker). Have a jukebox? This is the room for it. Your chairs should be silver and vinyl with an optical-illusion pattern. And to top it off, a sign that says EAT HERE is perfect for a room that says "Eat Here."

If you're not a patty-melt person, a formal dining room will create a formal place for funkiness in your home. Start with a podium for the imaginary maitre d' and add big gold-framed oil paintings on every wall. (You can buy them anywhere, even gas stations.)

Left: Try a diner theme with a Blue Plate Special. "I'll have Adam and Eve on a raft and wreck it."

Get the china hutch out of there and replace it with a dessert cart with plastic pastry replicas on fancy lace doilies. You'll need mood music and mood lighting. The fire marshal might require you to place an EXIT sign over one of your doors. Now that's authentic. Dress up your chairs with velvet covers cinched with satin ribbon. Add menus with gold tassels for your guests. Then set your table in all-white linens with your best china and crystal stemware. Serve pizza and you're Wolfgang Puck!

If the china and silver you inherited is a hodgepodge of serving pieces and incomplete place settings, use one item from each china pattern and host a high-society girlie-girl tea party. Unwrap

the six different crystal candlesticks you got for wedding presents and place them, varying sizes and shapes, in the center of your table. Invite the girls over for high tea and mark each place card with their princess names like *Princess Renée* and *Princess Jeanne*. It's the perfect opportunity for you and your friends to wear your tiaras and sip tea from your grandmother's mismatched collection of teacups and saucers. For the utmost in fun, serve cupcakes instead of watercress sandwiches and take the whole shebang out of doors!

License for *Fun*:

Saving your finest china for a special occasion wards off the special occasions awaiting you at every meal. Sipping your chocolate milk from a Waterford Crystal goblet is fun.

Far left: Mismatched china sets the table for a Funky Shui tea party.

Top left: Any time you can wear a tiara is Funky Shui!

Top right: It's all about cupcakes.

Above: The joy of a home office, cushy chair, remote control, and all.

the **hOME**
OFFICE

All Work and No Play Makes This a Dull Room

Is your home office looking a little too much like an *office* office? Getting that cube-farm feeling in your own home? Time to get to work making your home office a place for serious fun. Manage your office's maximum-profit-flow through the discipline of Funky Shui. One of the great joys of working from home, aside from conference calls in your jammies, is creating your own workspace. Business before pleasure? We beg to differ. Give yourself a raise by applying the Four Fun-damental Directions of Funky Shui.

Find the Playful Center

Beyond the Bored Room

If your home office is a card table in the hallway with a shoebox full of papers, and you find yourself writing with an eraser-less pencil (that someone else has chewed on), it's time for a fun takeover. Your success-in-business energy cannot thrive while you sit in a metal folding chair at a makeshift desk. Working at home is finally your chance to have the corner office. And making your work-at-home space funky is fundamental to work-happiness and productivity.

The center of the home office is the desk. How much fun can a desk be? A whole lotta fun! Select a desk that suits your business needs and supports your *fun-ductivity*. A glass desk enhances clear thinking, while a desk made of oak keeps your thoughts firmly rooted to the ground. Don't like working at a desk? Put the phone by the La-Z-Boy and your laptop on a TV tray and you'll feel like you're watching baseball instead of covering your bases. Unusual office desks are the perfect acquisition for the Funky Shui home office. Use a surfboard as a desk to ride the economic wave while swimming with the sharks.

For many telecommuters, the computer is their window to the world. Create a shrine to this window by placing

candlesticks at either side of your monitor. An offering of paper-clips should be made each morning and each time the computer crashes. Transform a computer that is terminally beige by decoupaging its surface with Monopoly money. Create a merger of home and office energies by taping family photos to your monitor. Put your monitor on a lazy Susan to turn your company toward success.

Far left: This home office lets you surf the Web, literally.

Top left: Hang ten in your office while you swim with the sharks.

Above: Will you find success? *Ask again later.*

Make your office official by hanging out your "shingle" in the form of a real old-fashioned sign. Hang a big eye in your office if you're a private investigator. (Or even if you're not. We all have to do some sleuthing in our jobs, don't we?) An old Ma Bell sign over the phone is sure to bring warmth to cold calling. And every home office needs an OPEN/CLOSED sign. This lets you know when to quit having fun at work and start having fun at home.

Tired of running your home from a tiny nook in the kitchen? Then do what any innovative domestic engineer would do and take your office into the bathtub. Pay the bills, organize the coupons, and plan your master bath renovation while relaxing in

License for Fun:

Don't forget important reminder signs like ALL EMPLOYEES MUST WASH THEIR HANDS, EMPLOYEES ONLY, and HARD HAT AREA. You can't be too careful, even at home. You never know when those OSHA inspectors will drop by.

your own sudsy indoor pool. Since a regular tub tray is too small for so many projects, add an actual desk by placing a board across the tub. First, waterproof your desk by covering it with a vinyl tablecloth in your favorite color, then box up your office and take it to the tub. According to Funky Shui legend, working in water washes away workaholism because no one wants to work once the water's gone cold. Add sage bath foam for clear thinking and your tub home office will bubble with success.

Interoffice Memo:

Remember to change
your outgoing message to
"Rub-a-dub-dub, I'm workin'
in the tub!"

● ● ● ● ● ● ● ● ● ● ● ● ● ● ● ● ● ● ● ●

Far left: Paper clips. Shaken, not stirred.

Far right: A home office in the bathtub is strictly for Employees Only.

Above: Rub-a-dub-dub, I'm workin' in the tub.

It is also recommended that one name the home office. It's more exciting to work in an office called "Mission Control" than in "The Dungeon." Remember, the title you give your home office declares your company's mission to the universe.

Funky Shui Names for Your Home Office

The Laboratory

The West Wing

The Bridge

The Nerve Center

Un-Funky Shui Names for Your Home Office

> **The Sweatshop**
>
> **The Hole**
>
> **The Salt Mines**
>
> **The Penalty Box**

Ever feel like your job is a sitcom? Put yourself in the spotlight by trading your office chairs for a pair of director's chairs. Label the backs with a hilarious sitcom duo like *A. Taylor* and *B. Fife*. Feeling like work is a grind? Choose *F. Flintstone* and *B. Rubble*. Put a star on the door to your office and write your to-do list on a clapboard. Now, if only you had a laugh track . . .

Color Me Funky
Putting Color to Work

A home office with a brown desk in a white room is due for a color merger. You've probably asked yourself, "What color is my parachute?" Now it's time to ask yourself, "What color is my office?" Follow the Funky Shui Occupation Color Guide to add a spectrum of funkiness:

Colors That Increase Your Bottom Line

> ***The Color of Money:*** Increases health and wealth.
>
> ***Blue Chip:*** Invests in your good fortune.

Left: Make your home office a blockbuster production.

Above: This chair lets everyone know who's in charge.

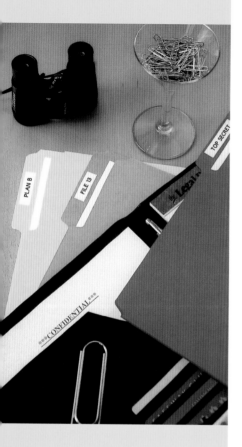

Gold Standard: Encourages you to go for the gold.

Yellow Pages: Improves clarity of mind and phone.

Negative Colors for Your Bottom Line

Pink Slip: Decreases company morale.

Bored Room Gray: Leave this tedious color at the corporate office.

In the Red: Could create a liability.

Blackmail: Keep your business out of this dark alley.

Where else can you go with color in your home office? To the moon! Or at least to your file cabinet. Those red, green, and yellow file folders are a must for the Funky Shui filer. And with an automatic label machine, your file names themselves can participate in the fun. "Accounts Payable?" Why not "Chump Change"? Or how about "Secret Plan" instead of "To-Do List"? And don't forget to label a file folder "Plan B." (It's important to always have a Plan B.) Got ordinary metal file cabinets? Spray paint them. In the Funky Shui home office, your filing should keep you smiling.

Have a happy day from nine to five in a Smiley Face Office. Paint your monitor yellow and surround your computer with miles of smiles. Those perennial icons of the good mood come in everything from pencil-toppers to penholders. A smiley face mouse pad spreads joy to your spreadsheet. Get a happy face clock, too. As long as you're going to be watching the clock, it might as well be smiling back at you. Good times.

Other areas to put color to work in your Funky Shui office

Above: Label your files whatever you want! (It's important to always have a Plan B.)

Opposite left: This home office is sure to make you whistle while you work.

Opposite right: Have a happy day every day in a Smiley Face home office.

Following page: A two-foot-tall lightbulb lamp is a great idea!

abound. Get yourself a white board with pens the colors of the rainbow. You'll need a pen cup, too. (How about an old SPAM tin? SPAM not only tastes funky, it is funky!) Fill it with souvenir pens from your travels. (A Statue of Liberty pen can be so liberating.) Prefer pencils? Break out your colored pencil set and do your first draft in periwinkle. Get your clients on the same page by using colored staples, a sure way to make them smile, even at an invoice.

Funky Shui Fortune:

Working at the end of a rainbow guarantees you a pot of gold.

Enlighten-up

Funky Lighting That Works

Funky Shui lighting at work will bring enlightenment to your bottom line. Don't settle for a dormitory desk lamp, when the light that it shines illuminates very little. Instead choose a two-foot-tall lightbulb lamp to represent all your great ideas.

Feeling stressed while you work? Get yourself a relaxing Lava Lamp. In the office? Why not? It's your space. Every room can use a string (or ten) of twinkle lights. Select lights that suit your business. For public relations, how about little telephones?

Landscape architect? Potted plant string-lights. Accountant? Dollar-sign lights. Want to go for broke? Light up the sky with rented movie premier lights to announce your new office. Okay, maybe that's too much for a home office, but now that two-foot-tall lightbulb is starting to sound reasonable, isn't it?

Your home office should have a view and lots of natural light, as the sun's rays are key for enlightenment. Does your office window look out on the neighbor's trash cans? Create a view of your own by painting a mural. Take your office to the beach with a photo of the Riviera. Or put your home office on Wall Street with a painting of the Manhattan skyline. If you don't feel like Michelangelo, frame a poster of a scenic destination and hang curtains on each side. Add a shelf as a windowsill to complete the window effect. Your home office can have a view of Kensington Palace or Hearst Castle. Who knew you had such famous neighbors?

Abundance Through Abundance
Your Cube Away from Work

Go to any large company and even some small ones and you'll find the cube-farm. A labyrinth of gray-carpeted dividers that make their occupants feel like trapped rats. (Feel better about working at home yet?) And what do those cooped-up employees do to their cube walls to escape the sameness, dreariness, and dullness of their corporate workspaces? They hang up comic strips. Your home office is your cube away from work. You, too, can hang up comic strips, print out funny e-mails, and display family photos. It's one of the joys of the office, home or high-rise. So go for it!

Give your office a higher degree of fun with framed certificates. Didn't graduate Magna Cum Laude from Harvard Business School? How about framing your Ed McMahon Publisher's Clearinghouse Certificate? (You may already be a winner.) You can make

License for *Fun*:

Hold a business card drawing every day and you'll always be a winner.

License for *Fun*:

An old vending machine that dispenses pencils, pens, and paperclips dispenses fun. (Make it free so you don't have to dig in the sofa for change.)

Far left: A SPAM can makes a great pencil holder for direct marketers.

your own mock degrees on the computer, like *Master of Fun Arts, Beauty School Dropout,* or *Employee of the Month*. Frame that *Good Behavior at the Dentist's Office* certificate you got when you were five or your *Perfect Attendance* certificate from Camp Winnebago. If anyone actually reads your "diplomas," they'll get a solid dose of fun. (When you complete this book, be sure to grant yourself a *Doctorate of Funky Shui*.)

Don't play it safe with blue and white safety checks from the bank when dozens of check designs are available to bring you abundance and *fun-lightenment*. And don't sign your checks with a faux Mont Blanc that has your old company's name rubbing off on the side. That's not Funky Shui. That's depressing. Use a fuzzy

KEY TO SUCCESS & BATHROOM

troll pen or a pink ballpoint that smells like bubblegum. A scented pen is just what you need for that sweet smell of success. Use an eraser shaped like a bear to erase ideas that are unbearable.

Make your money business funny business. While you're filling out your checks, imagine what fun you can have with that pesky memo line. Share your favorite recipes, Seinfeld quotes, or elephant jokes with the power company. Pass along the fun and they'll thank you for brightening their day.

The Funky Shui office is both fun and functional. Creative storage and clever labels lay the groundwork for

Far left: Writing with travel pens guarantees you're going places.

Left: Signage is *key* in your home office.

prosperity. Store your files in a wall of old post-office boxes. Label each mailbox with the names of the made-up employees you grumble at throughout your day. Who sorts the mail? Miss Handler. Who does the typing? Ellem N. Opee. Who makes travel arrangements? Lois Fair. A wall of school lockers is a smart way to organize your office supplies. Pencils, extra paper, and boxes of paper clips need a tidy place of their own to prevent an office-supply revolt.

The Funky Shui Dress Code states, "Every day is casual Friday." A plush chenille bathrobe is fine but how about a glamorous smoking jacket? And faxing in boxers is one of the seven secrets of highly funky people. Wear a nametag in the home office as a reminder to always be your *self*. Better yet, lock up your office each night so you can open it in the morning with your "keys to success." And as you duck out early on a Friday afternoon and travel your short commute home from your home office, be thankful that the only boss you have to watch out for is you.

Rule of Fun:

When you work at home, every day is "Take your pet to work day."

An Altar to Love

Surrounding yourself with the elements of Funky Shui in the bedroom titillates the Love Muse and enhances romance. Your *Romeo Mojo* needs a divine chamber to set free the love-giving forces of the universe. Plus it's fun to have a boudoir dedicated to the three elements of romance: love, passion, and mood lighting, of course. To create your altar to love, apply the Four Fun-damental Directions of Funky Shui.

Find the Playful Center

A Bed of Roses

According to eons of Funky Shui lore, the Master Bed is the playful center of the master bedroom, and one can guess why. For Funky Shui Practitioners, bed placement in the master bedroom is critical to enhancing love within the bedroom. When positioning the bed, do not place the headboard directly against a wall, as boring bed placement leads to boring bed play (but a bed that is catawampus could lead to cuddlyrumpus!). A headboard that rests against a wall acts as a percussive instrument that disrupts harmony (and could lead to embarrassment) in love.

Leave the bedroom door open to enhance exhibitionism. Closet doors should remain closed at all times, because *clothes* and *closed* live in harmony. To prevent your love from roaming, place

seven lucky flattened pennies in a felt-lined box under the right side of the bed. This small box represents your love, so protect it with a winged heart to keep your love and your lucky pennies from taking flight. This ritual has a 99.7 percent effectiveness rate that is directly related to your belief in its effectiveness. In Funky Shui, the creation of a ritual is fun!

It is a myth that the size of your playful center doesn't matter, so your bed should definitely not be twin-sized. Single beds may be playful as a reminiscence of childhood, but, despite the duplicative name, two in a twin is not

twice the fun. Instead, choose a queen-size bed for royal snuggling. For more elbow room (and knee room), the regal king-size bed can lessen negative friction while maintaining positive friction. Forgo the gargantuan California king, because a bed with two zip codes fails to deliver love's zip. Not everything bigger is better.

Consider the message your headboard is sending. A sleigh bed says, "Take me away." A country charmer with heart-shaped cutouts says, "Hee-haw, let's have some fun, little filly!" A canopy bed is a magic carpet ride that brings fantasy and mystery to your room's playful center. A garden gate headboard opens the door to your secret garden. An upholstered headboard says, "Don't worry, you won't get hurt."

The type of bed you select can determine whether you're snuggling in comfort or bunking alone. Adjustable beds aren't just for hospitals any more; extreme comfort while sitting, lounging,

Rule of *Fun*:

Take care to remove books from sight in the bedroom that could contradict positive love flow. Books with titles like *Impotent No More* and *Women Who Love the Wrong Men* should be placed in the bottom drawer of your dresser with your "back massager."

Love Note:

A single white rose bud in a glass vase represents chastity—so you don't have to.

Opposite left: Lucky pennies make you lucky in love.

Opposite right: Think outside the box spring. A garden gate makes a blooming-good headboard.

Left: Kiss by the book in a Romeo and Juliet Bedroom.

Following page: A Romeo and Juliet Bedroom is the height of romance. Just don't drink the poison!

or reclining is definitely part of a Funky Shui bedroom. A gothic wrought-iron four-poster sends a message of adventure and abandon. Bunk beds are perhaps the only style of bed clearly not recommended for the Funky Shui master bedroom (unless that suits your particular fantasy).

Color Me Funky

The Color of Love

Walls of the bedroom should be painted in bold colors to reflect the intensity of your love. Get yourself in the mood by getting your room in the mood with carefully selected hues.

Paint Away Bad *Mojo* with These Dreamy Colors

Blue Heaven: Lifts you to Cloud Nine.

Moonstruck: This silvery shade takes your love to Lookout Point.

Red Hot: Makes your passion sizzle.

Afternoon Delight: This bright yellow asks, "Why wait until the sun goes down?"

Colors That Smother Your Good *Mojo*:

Envy: It's not easy being green.

Ice Box: This color could lead to a chilly reception.

Jaded: A color that could use an attitude adjustment.

Scarlet Letter: Especially bad for married couples.

For more color fun, crowd out the bed bugs with a menagerie of throw pillows in colors that accent your internal hues of love. Pillows embroidered with Xs and Os can be rearranged for fun and thrills. (XXX and OOO!) A bed without colorful throw pillows is like a slumber party for one, not Funky Shui. Cushion the body and you cushion the soul—and the soul is the center of joy and love.

To encourage romantic play winter, spring, summer, and fall, choose bedclothes that are "your color" (see Carole Jackson's 1987 book, *Color Me Beautiful*). Looking your best in bed will make you lucky in love. You'll be a "10" in a bedroom dressed to the nines. Try a color theme like red with roses, midnight blue with dreamy stars, or romantic purple with playful polka dots. Can't make up your mind? How about a Twister bedspread and sheets? (Right Hand Red!)

A bedroom with drab shades seems like visiting Grandma's, but a bedroom with bright, billowing silk curtains is a fantasy from a romance novel. Flowing, colorful window treatments transport the love of the universe into the love of the bedroom. Try white gauzy sheers for a dreamy room or red velvet for a sultry room. A swag adds a swagger to your lover's step. A valance adds balance, which is important when acrobatics come into play.

The Light of Your Life

One candle is a lonely beacon but one hundred candles ignite the sacred internal flames of passion. Placing candles of multiple colors and shapes on the bedside table adds pleasing variety to your love life (important after years of marriage). And the warm glow of candlelight is flattering to all skin tones. Try scented candles. (Buttercream Frosting is the official scent of Funky Shui. There is

Rule of *Fun*:

While the bedroom should be a shrine to your heart's desire, making it a shrine to a fantasy lover prevents true love from entering. A Romeo and Juliet bedroom is Funky Shui; a Leonardo DiCaprio bedroom is not.

Right: A naked lampshade shines a naked light. Trim a lamp with boa feathers to increase your *Romeo Mojo.*

Far right: Leave your lover sweet invitations to promote harmony, happiness, and romance.

no room that would not benefit from this scent.) Votives, sconces, and dramatic candelabra work equally well to let your love-light fill the room. Candle-sconces flanking a mirror reflect the light of your love and passion. The element of passion lives in the tender flicker of a flame. Do not burn a candle out, for the flame that flickers out in life, flickers out in love.

A lampshade without fringe or tassels shines a naked light. Adorn your lamps as you would your self, and your love-light will glow even brighter. Chinese silk scarves draped over a bedside lamp—shining no more than a forty-watt bulb—increase harmony while reducing shyness. For an added harmonious glow, place a light on the floor behind an eight-foot

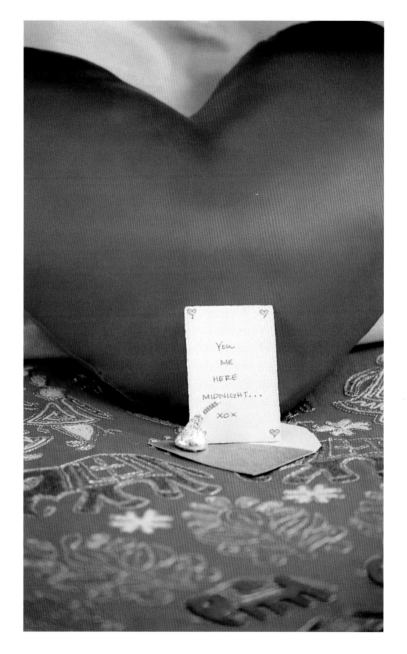

Rule of *Fun*:

Do not literally carry a torch in the bedroom. Tiki torches belong outside. Romantic fabrics, while inflaming passion, are also known to be flammable. "Burning Down the House" is a funky song, but it's not Funky Shui.

Love Note:

Lava lamps in the bedroom let the love flow.

Funambulism:

The blue light emanating from the TV walks a fine line between entertainment and distraction. If you end up watching Letterman and Leno instead of tending to your lover, then the TV may not belong in your Altar of Love.

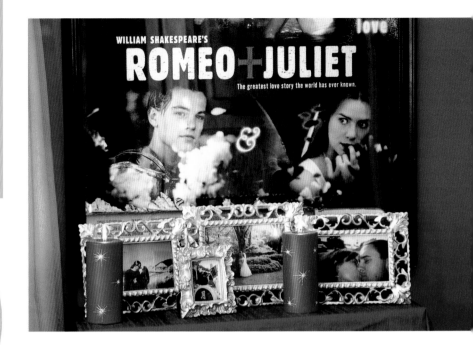

Schefflera tree. The dancing shadows this creates on your ceiling enhance the love-energy through their sensual movement. If the shadows are not dancing, give the tree a jiggle.

Light your playful center by placing matching lamps on bedside tables to the right and left of the master bed. Bedside lamps not only provide a guiding light for you and your lover as you travel down the path of life together, they also illuminate your favorite book. There are few activities better in the world of Funky Shui than cuddling up with a good book. Recommended bedroom reading includes Mystery and Romance.

A mirror is a powerful tool for energy-flow, so its placement requires the utmost precision and care. The bedroom mirror must be positioned on the wall farthest from the door and should hang at exactly the same height as the bed to shine your love back to you, thus doubling its sensual power. (Keep in mind that some angles are better than others!) A mirror that reflects a closet door reflects a closeted love.

Abundance Through Abundance
Love Me, Love My Stuff

Shower your love life with rows of roses for luck in love. Hang no fewer than twenty-five silk roses, flower-side down, from the

Left: A room by any other name would smell as sweet.

Below: A honeymoon theme makes the consummate master bedroom.

Above: Say "I do" to a Honeymoon Bedroom.

Top right: Toss the dice and have some fun!

Far right: The bells are ringing for these love birds.

ceiling in five evenly spaced rows. When you wake up to a sky of flowers, every day is Valentine's Day. While roses are the work-horses of the love-flower connection, wildflowers conjure up images of lovers running toward one another with open arms.

To heighten the drama, embrace a theme. A Romeo and Juliet bedroom says, "Did my heart love till now?" A bedroom with a balcony can lend itself to romantic role-play. (Just don't drink the poison.) A brothel theme for your bedroom may seem like a good idea as it invokes lust and abandon, but it may also invoke suspicion. (Remove the MASTERCARD ACCEPTED sign from the window with a razor blade and a little Goo-Gone.)

Photos of you and your lover kissing should be placed throughout the room in small frames. The gentle touching of lips represents the tenderness of the soul, and kissing photos seal your tender soul with a kiss. A framed love letter is art from the heart. Place a cherished love poem from your dearest in a gilded frame, and every year will be your golden anniversary. If you're not a poet (and you know it), frame a favorite poem from a master. Don't love Browning, Byron, or Yeats? Then frame the lyrics of "your song" or a favorite film quote about love. And for a daily play on words, leave love notes under your lover's pillow—sweet nothings lead to sweet somethings. Add a Hershey's Kiss to foreshadow your sweet desires.

Celebrating ten years of marriage? Why not renew your vows every night in the Honeymoon *Sweet*. Create an altar to your special day using your bride and groom cake topper, toasting glasses, and tiered wedding-cake candles. Shower your white-and-aqua boudoir with your wedding pictures on the bedside table and a lampshade draped with your wedding veil. Frame your wedding invitation or the sweetest lines of your wedding vows. Place a "Just Married" banner over the marital bed and create a reason for foofy lingerie every night.

Below: Pictures of Rick and Ilsa will spice up this gin joint as time goes by.

Bottom: What Casablanca Bedroom is complete without a Fez Monkey?

Right: A Casablanca theme is the beginning of a beautiful bedroom.

Far right: Here's looking at you, kid.

To infuse a relationship with adventure, create a Casablanca Room. Round up the usual un-Funky Shui suspects: the floral bed-in-a-bag comforter, the dusty fake ficus, and the stack of weight loss books. You must remember this: These do not belong

Funambulism:

A frivolous mosquito net is romantic. A mosquito net required to keep your delicates from getting bitten is unromantic. Try a citronella candle instead.

in your Casablanca Room. Start the love recirculating with a slow-sweeping ceiling fan. Between you and me and the lamppost, bringing a street lamp indoors brings a romantic glow back into the bedroom. Finally, hanging mosquito netting over the bed will make you both want to play it again.

If your bedroom is your place to get away, you should take yourself away on a trip. Funky Shui is your passport to decorate your bedroom in whatever place and time you choose. So why not make it Paris in the springtime? Put an Eiffel Tower lamp on your bedside table, blue-and-white *jolie* toile fabric on the bed, soaps from Marseilles, and voilà! Your bedroom will give you a mini-vacation every night. Bon Voyage!

Far left: *Ooh La La!* This French bedroom has that je ne sais quoi.

Above: Counting sheep just got easier. There are six.

Left: *Parlez-vous* Funky Shui?

The Dragon and the Bedroom:

Don't live on the back of the Dragon, wear a dragon on your back in the form of a silk kimono. Hang the kimono dragon-side-out on the back of the bedroom door. Keeping the Dragon on your back keeps you off his.

Above: A giant fortune cookie brings giant good fortune.

Right: Don't live on the back of the Dragon, wear a dragon on your back—the back of your silk kimono.

Funky Shui = Funky + Water

The loo, the water closet, or the powder room. No matter what you call it, the bathroom is your personal sanctuary. The bathroom is the center for your spiritual and literal cleansing. Creating a spa in the home cultivates calmness within the household and cleanses the home of negativity in the form of personal dirt. Lather up your creativity using the Four Fun-damental Directions of Funky Shui.

Find the Playful Center

Tiny Bubbles

The playful center of your bathroom is not only the largest item in the room, but it's also the vessel to your *center*—the bathtub. Like The Fridge, the positioning of the bathtub is preordained and we must not doubt the placement proficiency of the Tub Titans. A standard porcelain tub is a clean slate for your wildest dreams. By simply adding water, your spiritual goals become the soup of destiny in which you simmer. A claw-foot tub stands on high alert to protect your destiny from the Dragon. To reach the serenity summit, sink into a Jacuzzi bathtub because, well, a tub with its own bubbles is the ultimate in Funky Shui. Solitude is lonely, but a Jacuzzi bathtub built for two is fun! A

Funky Shui Fortune:

A bubble is a wish, and when it pops, your wish is released into the Universe.

bubbling bath has a life of its own and as the bubbles of that life bounce off you, extra energy is added to your world.

Bubbles and water are the two most important elements of Funky Shui bathroom balance. Funky Shui literally means "funky" and "water" (seriously, it does); therefore, funkiness within water is key to paying homage to the Funky Shui gods. A luxurious bath is

Right: This spa bathroom whispers gentle reminders. Laugh, smile, and relax.

Far right: You're never alone when you bathe with Mr. Bubble.

The Tao
of *Fun*:

Good clean fun starts
with "good" and "clean."
(And ends with fun!)

an elixir that washes away the blues. And a home with bubbles is a home that effervesces love. For unfettered fun, pour Mr. Bubble into your bath while blowing bubbles. Top this off with a loungey version of "Tiny Bubbles" (can it ever be un-loungey?) and you've achieved the Tub Trifecta. Truly bubblicious.

Loosen up with light reading material (like an airplane novel, the *Big-X Crossword,* and a tabloid or two). Light reading lightens

Rule of *Fun*:

Fill the tub and turn off the faucet before stepping into the water. This allows the tumultuous water flow to calm itself so it is free to calm you.

the mind and spirit. Browse while bathing by flipping through your favorite catalogs. Who needs a personal shopper when you can shop in the tub? Don't forget your eye-cooling mask, nail polish, and a nice spritzer with a sprig of mint.

If your bathroom does not have a tub, fear not. The playful center of a tubless bathroom is the *shower,* your own personal waterfall. Cascading water washes away negativity and cleanses your spirit. Soap-on-a-Rope, called *Savon du Cord* in French, is a Funky Shui talisman for spiritual and physical purification. The shape of a heart promotes love, the shape of a lily promotes purity, and the shape of a microphone promotes singing in the shower. Add a shower radio for shower-

karaoke and dance with abandon to intensify this effect. (Serenade yourself with an old shower-standard like "Soap Gets in Your Eyes.")

Color Me Funky

Powder Room in Bloom

The walls of your bathroom need color to awaken your dormant energy and allow your spirit to flourish. And a small room like the bathroom is the perfect place to take a giant step (Mother, may I? Yes, you may.) toward your ultimate Funky Shui goal.

Choose These Hues for a Serene Sanctuary

Serenity Sage: Soothes the soul and spirit.

Eucalyptus: Botanical colors encourage you to turn over a new leaf every day.

Mimosa: Pale colors tickle the senses for the ultimate in rejuvenation.

Lavender and Lemongrass: Complementary colors compliment you.

Flush These Colors Down the Drain

Mildew: Creates a quagmire that could trap your Chi.

Creature from the Black Lagoon: Beware of this murky color scheme.

Slime: Makes your relaxation zone a danger zone.

Soap Scum: An unclean tub fogs your spirit.

Far left: Celebrate your manicure with a shrine to the Rainbow of Enamels.

Once your walls are painted, additional color can be added and changed easily by updating the smaller, decorative, and practical items in your bathroom like towels, bath mats, shower curtains, and tchotchkes. Your Funky Shui bathroom will be warm and fuzzy with the addition of shag bath mats. Warm your soul from the toes up with soft and fluffy rugs. But don't robe the entire toilet with a lid rug, a tank rug, and a rug around the base. A fully carpeted commode is a little too much like a '70s van; you don't want to *go* there.

The addition of a festive and protective shower curtain increases inspiration for funky bathroom decoration, while decreasing soggy bath mats. Fill the pockets of a clear vinyl curtain with pennies to

shower yourself with wishes in your own private Trevi Fountain. A school-of-goldfish shower curtain makes the day go swimmingly. A curtain of cats and dogs portend the coming shower (just don't step in a poodle). A curtain displaying a map of the world opens your world to travel and international fame and fortune.

For the ultimate in relaxation with a splash of color, focus on nurturing the key elements of your *self:* body, mind, and soul. (Ooh, and toes!) To properly nourish the body, mind, soul, and toes, include the following colorful items in your daily ablutions, prefer-

Far left: Fall in love with a heart-themed bathroom.

Above: A tincture of Tickle Tonic is just for giggles.

ably displayed in an inviting way in a decorative tub tray or rattan tub-side basket:

Fun-Shaped Soaps: Pink hearts, yellow moons, orange stars, and green clovers are the Lucky Charms of cleansing. Ideal for your serenity cereal.

Bath Beads: Multicolored aromatic beads soften both your skin and your outlook on life. It's like poetry in lotion.

Tub Tea: Chai calms your Chi, comfrey makes you comfy. Invite Earl Grey to join you so you won't be lonely.

A Dangling Plant: Plants love the warm, moist environment of a bath-room, and a thriving plant circulates positive energy flow. Plus it's pretty.

Enlighten-up

Mirror Mirror on the Wall

Flattery will get you everywhere and that is especially true in the Funky Shui'd bathroom. A mirror is a reflection of you—of every decision you've made, every experience you've had, and every giggle you've giggled. Look to your mirror to show you at your best and it will protect your outer and inner beauty. But a mirror that hangs in front of a toilet reflects your spirit into the plumbing and washes it down the drain. Pore-enlarging mirrors must be banished from all Funky Shui bathrooms.

A nightlight is a beacon to those who might need to find their way in the dark. Choose a nightlight that speaks to the mood of the room, for that small light is the room's only representative after hours. Try a scalloped seashell for a seaside bathroom. The classic crescent moon nightlight is ideal for your turn-of-the-century outhouse look. A peace sign is perfect for a retro '70s theme, and add a lava lamp to your *lava*tory to make it *dy-no-mite*.

The Funky Shui bathroom is bathed in candlelight. And in this room, there is no such thing as going overboard. A candlescape that rests on the cistern encourages positive energy flow and wicks away dead energy. Twelve tea-lights standing along your windowsill stand guard against the Dragon's own fire.

Rule of *Fun*:

Give your spirit and your face a lift by looking at yourself in a hand mirror while tilting your head back toward the southernmost point of your home. A Funky Shui Facelift lifts your face and your spirits.

Far left: This ritual will help you follow your heart and cleanse your soul.

Above: The Funky Shui candlescape. (Just don't add water.)

Floating candles bathe you in a soothing glow of lightness and clarity. Aromatherapy candles ignite abundance for the ultimate in bathroom serenity and spa fun. Try patchouli to feel grounded, clove to spice up your love life, and vanilla so you can have your cake and eat it, too. Myrrh promotes mystery, peppermint refreshes, and Coast deodorant soap is an eye-opener.

Abundance Through Abundance

Bathroom Bric-a-brac

Use bathroom bric-a-brac, like soaps, soap dishes, and toothbrush holders, to theme your water closet for the ultimate in good clean fun. A theme for your bathroom can help your powder room bloom in ways you may not have considered before:

Hearts-a-Flutter: Wear your heart on your sleeve in your bathroom and your love life will take flight. Surround yourself with the symbols of love to let the universe know you're available for romance. Heart-shaped soaps, candles, throw rugs, and string-lights make this room dance to its own pulsing beat. Drying off with *His* and *Hers* embroidered towels rubs the spirit with jealousy and possessiveness. Instead wrap yourself in bath towels embellished with fun words like *Love*, *Happiness*, *Dry Me*, or *Slippery When Wet*. What to wear in the Funky Shui bathroom? Your birthday suit if it

Opposite top: Pets are the Official Mascot of Funky Shui.

Opposite bottom: The couple that brushes together stays together. (And kisses more!)

Left: A boat-themed bathroom says "Welcome Aboard."

Above: Looks like the catch of the day is Charmin.

WELCOME ABOARD

suits you. Or try big fluffy hotel-type robes with big fluffy slippers. If you work from home you can wear them all day.

The Head: This nautical theme is every sailor's dream, only without the cramped quarters, rolling seas, and pirate attacks. Hang towels from small anchors, use trout-shaped soaps, and make a mini-mast for your bathtub. Why not hang a faux marlin over the tub? That's a great way to reel in the Dragon.

The Can-Can: This Parisian-inspired room will make your guests say, "*Oui oui.*" To kick up the fun, turn your Can-Can into a brothelesque dressing room from the Moulin Rouge, with red brocade fabric draped from the ceiling, black lace curtains and a row of round bulbs down your mirror. Sign autographs from your velvet vanity chair, even if they're only for the bills.

The Luau Loo: Ocean blue walls with palm tree curtains are the perfect backdrop for leafy tropical plants, vibrant beach towels, and coconut candles. Make it an energizing island oasis decorated in red, turquoise, and yellow. Hang ten with ten leis, a tiki toothbrush holder, and a pineapple soap dish. Sing along with Don Ho to "Hawaiian Lullaby," while soaps that smell of mango, banana, and papaya do the hula in your nose. Add a tiki god and a collection of vintage hula-girl nodders and this room will say *Aloha* whether you're coming or going.

The Fountain of Youth: Words like *Dream* and *Smile* fashioned from armature wire dress up your tiles. Keep your pink cotton

The Dragon and the Bathroom:

You'll never have to fight the Dragon for your turn in the bathroom. The Dragon hates to get wet. It puts out his fire. Plus it ruins his hair.

Opposite top: Four out of five dentists recommend this funky toothbrush holder.

Opposite bottom: A life preserver towel rack rescues your bathroom from the Bermuda Triangle of Bad Taste.

Left: Have a luau in the loo. Oh, *poi!*

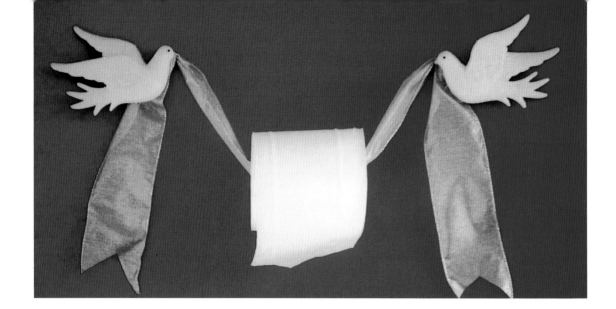

balls in an oversized glass. Bath oils and shower gels invoke fun and may cast a spell when kept in containers labeled *Tickle Tonic* and *Love Potion*. Line your tub with a hundred small candles as a thousand points of light and an offering to the goddess of feeling young.

What to Name Your Funky Shui Bathroom

The Studio

The Wishing Well

The Throne Room

The Oval Office

What Not to Name Your Funky Shui Bathroom

The John

The Crapper

The Potty

The Litter Box

Above: Get carried away with a *dovely* toilet paper holder.

Wish You Were Here

So you're lucky enough to have an extra bedroom for guests. Or do you think it is unlucky since you have to decorate yet another room? Have no fear, Funky Shui is here. And decorating a room for a weary traveler is your passport to fun. The guest room is much more than just a dry corner for your friends to hang their hats and rest their heads. It's their home away from home. Give your guests the greatest room in the house and they'll be glad they didn't stay at the local Hokey Hotel. Take your guests on a surprise trip in your home. (Keep your guests from getting lost by posting a mileage sign in your central hallway showing the direction and distance to each room.) When it comes to guest rooms, think *vacation* and start with the Four Fun-damental Directions of Funky Shui.

Find the Playful Center

Vacation Land

The playful center of your guest room is a Vacation Theme. Why? Vacations are Funky Shui. Where would you like your guest room to take you and your guests? So many options. The world is your oyster, so think big and make every item in the room look like a memento from your latest trek through exotic locales.

Top Travel Destinations for Your Guest Room

- **Alpine Ski Lodge**
- **The Copacabana**
- **The Love Boat**
- **Arabian Nights**

Restrict Travel to These Themed Guest Rooms

- **Roach Motel**
- **The YMCA**
- **Bus Depot**
- **Turkish Prison**

Your guests will say *"Veni, vidi, vavoom!"* when they see your Roman Temple guest room. All roads lead to fun in a room even Caesar would like. Line the room with ten white plaster columns and ten urns overflowing with ivy. Hang an "ancient" pediment over the bed with the phrase *Mea casa tea casa est* (literally, *Mi casa es su casa*). To truly make your guests feel like gods and god-

desses, leave out togas (this one is easy—they're just sheets). If they complain about the accommodations, remind them that your Roman Temple wasn't built in a day.

"This room rocks!" is what your guests will say when they stay in your Rock 'n' Roll Room. Give your friends and family a backstage

Far left: With a sign like this, your guests won't have to ask, "Which way to the bathroom?"

Left: This guest room rocks!

Above: Give your guests a backstage pass to the coolest room in the house.

pass to funkiness by hanging your electric guitar collection on the wall. Graffiti a wall with lyrics to your favorite rock songs. Golden Oldies like "The Wanderer," "Jailhouse Rock," and "Rock Around the Clock" will take your guests back in time. Or try classic rock stand-bys like "Freebird" and "Born to Run." "Hotel California" may be overdone, but if it's a favorite, it's Funky Shui. Don't

Encore:

Don't be surprised if your guests love your Rock 'n' Roll Room so much that they book a return engagement.

Right: Wow, a can of gold spray paint and you just sold 500,000 records!

forget to hang framed gold records on the wall. A few old vinyl albums from the thrift shop, a can of gold spray paint, and *ta-da*! You just sold 500,000 records!

To really get your guests into the vacation rhythm, turn your Rock 'n' Roll Room into an Elvis Tribute with a mock pilgrimage to the King's castle. In Graceland, as in Funky Shui, restraint is a dirty word. To achieve style fit for the King, you must go well outside your normal boundaries by placing two white ceramic greyhounds at the foot of the bed. Make your guests say "Hey, baby" by providing rhinestone-encrusted capes for them instead of robes. Write your favorite lyric from "Teddy Bear" and leave it on the bed with a room-service menu featuring peanut butter and banana sandwiches.

The Dragon and the Guest Room:

Word has it the Dragon is a big Elvis fan, so a Funky Shui tribute to the King makes you, your guests, and the Dragon happy.

For more adventures in decorating and travel, fly across the pond to jolly old England. A London Flat guest room sports a Union Jack bedspread and a classic Underground sign that reminds your guests to *mind the gap*. No carpet? Paint white stripes across the floor like Abbey Road. Put a sign over a grandfather clock that says "Big Ben" and have it chime on the quarter hour for authenticity. Refer to your backyard as Hyde Park. (Where can you get one of those red phone booths?) If your visitors turn out to be exemplary houseguests, you can knight them in the room's Westminster Abbey Corner.

Room Service:

Your Funky Shui guest room may become so popular you are constantly inundated with guests. If this happens, place a Room Rate card on the back of the door charging $200 a night with an 8:00 A.M. checkout time.

Local Color

Paint the walls, paint the ceiling, paint a mural. Inviting your friends into a colorful Funky Shui room brings new life to their love of travel. All you have to do is take a moment to choose the colors that best represent your destination theme. Greece is white and blue with a triglyph frieze around the crown molding. Paris is red, blue, and white. Or should we say "*rouge, bleu, et blanc*"? A cottage on South Beach is aqua and peach with a mural of the art deco skyline.

Have a Great Trip with These Vacation Colors

> **Canary Island:** All the fun without the sand in your suit.
>
> **Coral Reef:** Dive in for exotic adventure.
>
> **Purple Mountains Majesty:** Instantly creates a room with a view.
>
> **Gold Country:** Your relatives will feel like they hit the mother lode.

Don't Go There

> **Pepto-Bismol:** Pass on this queasy color scheme.
>
> **Yellow Fever:** Avoid it like the plague.
>
> **Sunburn:** This color is not a-peelin'.
>
> **Montezuma's Revenge:** Say *adios* to this nonpotable color scheme.

When you're through with the walls, let some color spill on the floor. Cover a bare floor with brightly colored throw rugs that go with the theme. Already have wall-to-wall carpeting? No reason you can't throw the rugs on top. That's why they call 'em throw rugs. Ten throw rugs shaped like pineapples spread the joy of hospitality to your guests ten times over. Create a garden where your guests can frolic by placing a variety of colorful flower-shaped rugs on the floor. If only you could let the butterflies in the house . . .

Left: Beach Blanket Bedroom!

Above: Your guests will dig this beach bungalow.

Themed Lamps Illuminate a Themed Room

Your guests will need bedside lamps to read by and perhaps an overhead to light their home away from home. Now for the fun. Since our theme for guest rooms is themes, lamps simply need to take their lead from the rest of the room.

Guide your guests to their seaside inn with a mini-lighthouse lamp. And if it's springtime in your guest room, you may want to add a bouquet of light-up tulips in a vase on the dresser. Ignite your Key West Fest Room with hurricane lamps. After your

Tourist Information:

A bare bulb hanging from the ceiling by a chain is a bad lamp for a guest room, as it may make your home seem like a flophouse.

guests check in, be sure to turn on your flashing neon *No Vacancy* sign at your Times Square Motel Room. When at a loss for lighting, remember, a sparkling chandelier can go in any room.

Rusty lanterns and a light-up stagecoach light the way to your Dude Ranch Guest Room. Invite the deer and the antelope to play with breezy open windows. Five horseshoes along the windowsill (open-end-up) bring your guests good luck. Stir up interest in your Western paperbacks with stirrup bookends and an antler lamp to

Opposite left: Round up your bottle cap collection and spur on the fun.

Opposite right: Howdy! Put your feet up and set a spell.

Left: An old suitcase gets new life in your Rodeo Rumpus Room. The stagecoach lamp stops here daily.

read by. This room says, "Put your feet up and stay awhile!"

If candles suit your themed guest room, all the better. Candles add mood lighting to your guest suite while stifling moodiness. But remember, fire is one of the four elements and must be handled with care. Provide an extinguisher and post an evacuation route on the back of the door for your guests. Now *that* is starting to feel like a real hotel.

Rule of Fun:

Mirrors in your guest room not only serve the purpose of helping your guest look his or her best, they also reflect light and circulate your guests' Chi so the room doesn't get too stuffy. But if it does, they can always open a window.

Abundance Through Abundance

Knock Knock! Knickknacks!

Outfit your guest room in its travel theme from stem to stern. What better place to showcase your travel souvenirs, maps, guide books, and vacation photos than in the guest room? Just be sure to select memorabilia that goes with your theme. Two rows of nesting Russian Matryoshka dolls and seven black lacquer boxes invite your guests back to the USSR. For a Turkish room, consider an embellished, camel-shaped ottoman and traditional

Opposite left: Your guests will *love* this Mexican-themed guestroom. Pass the margaritas!

Top left: Feeling hot, hot, hot!

Above: *Mi piñata es su piñata.*

Above: A minibar will make your guests feel like your place is the Ritz. If they outstay their welcome, start charging minibar prices.

Turkish rugs. Hang the evil eye you bought at the bazaar in Istanbul (or Pier One Imports) over the doorway to protect your guest's trip from ruin.

Say *hola* to a Hacienda Guest Room filled with hand-hammered tin candlesticks and handcrafted pottery from the

Mercado. Your guests can take a siesta on soft Mexican blankets while they fall asleep to Spanish language tapes. Use a chair as a bedside table to display silver picture frames. Provide the Aztec Calendar so your guests won't be late to the fiesta. All you need now is a piñata wearing a sombrero to shower your guests with *mucho* funky.

And now for some Funky Shui, just for your guests. Travel-size shampoos, lotions, and soaps are irresistibly fun, especially when they are displayed in a decorative basket or tin lunchbox (depending on your theme). You could have your mock hotel's name embroidered on some towels: the Ritz O'Neil, the Bradford Roadside Resort, or the Do-Drop-Inn. And why not make a friendly little free minibar. (Don't forget the Toblerone.) Set out local guidebooks and maps for your guests. And how about some stamped local postcards? A basket filled with travel magazines just screams, "I'm on vacation!"

Ticket to Fun:

Provide fluffy white robes for your guests to enhance their relaxation
while discouraging unwelcome exhibitionism.

The Dragon and the Guest Room: Don't let him overstay his welcome. Be sure to place a sign on the door that reads INVITED GUESTS ONLY.

PATRICK O'BRIAN   MASTER AND COMMANDER

A SEA OF WORDS

A LEXICON AND COMPANION FOR PATRICK O'BRIAN'S SEAFARING TALES

Don't Fence Me In

Whether your outdoor space is as big as all outdoors or it's just a container garden on a balcony, you can take the fun outside with Funky Shui. And when you take the fun outside, it can get pretty big. How big? Waterslide big. Roller coaster big. Merry-go-round big! Too big? Okay, maybe a little. Start with a simple Cleopatra lounge chair and apply the Four Fun-damental Directions of Funky Shui.

Find the Playful Center

What's Irish and sits by the pool? Patty O'Furniture.

A lawn chair is your front row seat for watching the grass grow. You can achieve harmony with nature while you attract joy and happiness to your neck of the woods if you look for the key element of Funky Shui exterior decorating—*the theme*. Choose a theme for your outdoor room and you can easily select the lawn furniture and decor to create your dreamscape.

While it can be satisfying to sit right down in the grass, you might be more comfortable becoming one with nature in a nice Adirondack chair. Put your feet up on a lobster trap and you've just transformed your everyday patio into a seaside getaway, even if you live in Missouri. Put on your

License for Fun :

A hammock in the backyard is a must for the Funky Shui napper, especially when it's a hammock-built-for-two.

Previous page: Enjoy seaside living even if you're landlocked.

Right: A hammock makes for a perfect afternoon snooze.

Far right: Create a living room outside for a cosmopolitan happy hour.

sunglasses and sunscreen. A pitcher of strawberry daiquiris later, you're sailing the seven seas in your own backyard. With Funky Shui and the out-of-doors, the sky is literally the limit.

Take your ordinary patio set to new heights of happiness with cushions in bright and fanciful oilcloth. (At oilcloth.com, their motto is "A new oilcloth makes the whole family happy.") If the pattern you choose has bananas on it, feel free to hang banana string lights around your gazebo. Green-and-white checks can create a sidewalk café right in your own backyard. Choose a giant sunflower motif to bring you sunshine no matter what the weather.

To extend your home out into nature, literally bring the inside out by creating a living room on nature's own shag carpet: grass. Arrange a sitting area with a rattan loveseat and chairs just like you would in your living room. But instead of facing the television, the seating should face your beautiful view, garden, or bird feeders to take advantage of Mother Nature's entertainment channel. Spend some time under the stars with a terra cotta outdoor fireplace to warm you during cool evenings. And spend the days communing with your outdoor pets: the bunnies, the birds, and the butterflies. Fresh and natural Funky Shui.

Color Me Funky

How Does Your Garden Grow?

Your outdoor space will flow with abundance of color and joy with nature's automatic joy enhancers—flowers. Like natural,

Funambulism:

Happy plants are Funky Shui. Dead plants are depressing. Throw them out, please. And water them next time!

Left: Your garden is always in bloom with these everlasting blossoms.

Above: Get a load of these garden delights.

 **Rule of *fun*:**

Lighting the path to your front door lights the path to your soul, as home is where the heart is.

- -

Above: Please don't eat the daisies.

Opposite left: Spinning away negative energy is a breeze with garden pinwheels.

Opposite right: Gosh, galoshes make great planters. Make sure they don't walk away!

ever-renewing tchotchkes, flowers bring color, whimsy, and joy into our yards. Garden not blooming? Fake it with fabulous plastic daisies. They're coming up everywhere! Too kitschy for your neighborhood? Try a trio of rusty lawn blooms. Gardens are ripe for funky decorating.

In the Funky Shui garden, more is more. Start with poppies but don't stop at just one. Seeing ten pots of popping poppies as you walk up your driveway will put a smile on your face after a hard day at work. Terra cotta pots are lovely, but if you want to have a field day, get creative with your containers.

For Funky Shui Gardening, Think Outside the Pot

Bathtub of Begonias

A Canoe of Cosmos

Cactus in a Cowboy Boot

Zinnias in a Toy Truck

Wildflowers in a Wagon

Plant some fun in and among your annuals. The flowerbed of your dreams has a headboard and a footboard with flowers planted like a quilt. Climb to new heights of funky by planting herbs between the rungs of a ladder lying on the ground. Put potted

Lawn Lore:

A Wishing Well
will wish you well.

Above: With Funky Shui, you can think outside the window box.

Opposite left: Looks like a bumper crop this year!

Opposite top: Label your vegetables so the bunnies can find them.

Opposite bottom: Nothing beats beets!

plants on the back step of a red tricycle. Laminated seed packets on Popsicle sticks give a garden that classic look and give you an instant green thumb. Create garden stakes that say "Weeds" to make everything growing in your flowerbed look intentional.

Let Fun Light the Way

In the daytime, the sun's rays dance with the butterflies, lighting the earth with mirth and helping your garden grow. But what happens after the sun goes down? Though tending your garden by moonlight may seem sublime, supplementing the moon's glow with practical outdoor lighting will help keep your home's evening-energy emanations from drifting into the cosmos. Footlights are not only an opportunity to adorn your sidewalk, but they also make the path in your life and to your door safer and more inviting. And not only for you, but also for your guests and the Dragon (now that he's become your friend in fun).

Extend light into the four corners of your lot in life to make your outdoor fun flourish after dark. To really make your garden grow, sprinkle twinkle lights on every tree and your yard will blossom

Right: Make wind chimes out of your silverware and you'll never have to polish it again.

Far right: Your home's name proclaims its spirit. For example, this home is Campy!

and grow with joy and happiness through the night. A row of flaming tiki torches turns a hot dog barbecue into a luau. String colorful Chinese lanterns along your fence to transport you to another time and place. Add smooth rocks, soft sand, and a rake, and you've got a Zen rock garden. Perfect for morning T'ai Chi or an afternoon cup of Chai Tea.

For a playful outdoor theme that will light up the neighborhood, cover the front walkway with red outdoor carpet for your award-winning home and your visitors will feel like movie stars. Set your motion-detector lights to flash like paparazzi as your guests approach the front door and make your doorbell a chorus of applause! Everyone loves the star treatment, especially when your neighbors are just

dropping by to return your hammer. (If you're feeling extra funky, create your own Neighborhood Walk of Fame, with a star for each member of the family. Sign your name and put your footprints in the cement. Don't forget your pets!)

Hang an enormous chandelier (if you have any left by now)

in the biggest tree you've got. To Funky Shui skeptics, a tree is a tree and a chandelier out-of-doors is an impossibility. But the Funky Shui Master can transform even the oldest tree into an outdoor chandelier by adorning it with glass fishing buoys, all the wind chimes you can find, Mexican tin ornaments, or mismatched garage sale silverware. Hanging offerings on the tree of life turns the wind into song. And not only that, you have permission to trim-a-tree all year long. (Tinsel-time!) Over time, the chimes, tin ornaments, or silverware will rust and sway in the wind, blowing good decorative vibes to your neighbors. They could probably use a little Funky Shui, couldn't they?

Garden Variety:

If you're more zany than Zen-y, turn your rock garden into a tribute to Florida in the '50s. Pink flamingos promote balance while encouraging play.

Abundance Through Abundance

Beyond the Garden Gnome

Statuary in the yard guards your home from the Winds of Negativity and keeps the Dragon company while you're away. Lawn sculpture comes in a variety of tastes and sizes, but the most effective lawn sentinels are big and hilarious. Maybe your neighbor has a tasteful sculpture of St. Francis of Assisi, a sweet terra cotta bunny, or a sandblasted stone that reads *Believe*. But with Funky Shui, you can throw caution to the wind and choose a big stucco Madonna in an upturned tub. Instant grotto! How about a supersized lawn chicken? Try a smattering of Easter Island heads. As long as you're going for large, how about nine holes of miniature golf? Check with the local zoning board to determine the allowable height for the dinosaur.

Don't hedge your bets by leaving your bushes naked; edge your hedge with a dozen pinwheels to spin away crabby neighbors. Got an old bottle collection? Border your garden with half buried bottles,

upside-down, for a sculptural, stained-glass effect. Paint ten old rural mailboxes in ten different colors and stake them across your lawn. A historical marker makes your yard a landmark. "Feline's Hill, site of the Great Cat Rebellion of 1986." Did you happen to find a rusty old letter "G"? Put it in the flowerbed by the geraniums to stand for *garden* and *green thumb*. And don't forget the *garden gnomes*. Remember more is more and five gnomes on the lawn bring five times the joy to all the snails that visit.

Above: Surround yourself with Funky Shui and you're on the road to *funlightenment!*

Outstanding Items for Your Yard

    Slip 'n' Slide

    Monkey Bars

    Trampoline

    Peacocks

Dreary Items for Your Yard

    Ford Pinto on Blocks

    Shopping Cart

    Real Gravestones

    Commode (unless you turn it into a koi pond)

A decorative doorknocker heralds playfulness by saying "Knock knock" in an interesting or silly way. "Who's there?" asks the brass woodpecker doorknocker, who tells your friends they've arrived at The Birdhouse. Don't forget to amuse those within your home with a doorbell that makes everyone smile. How about Beethoven's Fifth? If you rejoice at the sound of company coming, get a doorbell that plays the Hallelujah Chorus. Feeling festive? *La Cucaracha!* An echoing mansion doorbell gives your studio apartment stature. We've all heard the barking-dog doorbell, so why not a meowing-cat doorbell?

Before you can declare your home truly one with Funky Shui, you must name it. And you can welcome your guests with Funky Shui on their way to your front door with a decorative sign announcing the name of your estate.

Great Funky Shui Names for Your House

    Southfork

    The Taj

    Versailles

    Tara

Bad Funky Shui Names for Your House

The Doghouse

House of Cards

The Woodshed

The Rat's Nest

Pompeii

When your guests reach the entrance to your humble abode, welcome them with an expressive doormat. A traditional one says "Welcome," but a Funky Shui doormat teases your guests with what's inside. Humorous doormats abound, so avail yourself of one. And custom personalized doormats come in all shapes (well, mostly rectangular) and colors. Create your own mat that says "Mystery Spot" or "You are here." A Funky Shui doormat announces to all, "Let the games begin."

A Parting Gift

So you've Funky Shui'd your home. It's fun, fabulous, and your friends are lining up at the door. You've *enlightened-up* and you've gained abundance through abundance. How will you know when you're done? It's a common misperception in the world of Funky Shui to think that one might reach *funlightenment*. *Funfinity*. That you can make your home as funky as it could possibly be. Always keep in mind, with Funky Shui the journey is the reward. You can always find one more fun thing to do, one more funky thing to add that will liberate your playful side and fill your home with joy. So keep on the quest. Remember: Fun in your home is fun in your life. And everyone can use more of that.